ANIMALS UNDERGROUND
FOXES

EMILY SEBASTIAN

PowerKiDS press

New York

For Hannah, who has a fondness for foxes

Published in 2012 by The Rosen Publishing Group, Inc.
29 East 21st Street, New York, NY 10010

First Edition

Editor: Amelie von Zumbusch
Book Design: Julio Gil

Photo Credits: Cover, back cover (armadillo, fox, mongoose), pp. 4–5, 9, 13, 15, 18–19, 24 (bottom left, bottom right) Shutterstock.com; back cover (badger) Norbert Rosing/National Geographic/Getty Images; back cover (chipmunk) James Hager/Robert Harding World Imagery/Getty Images; back cover (mole) Geoff du Feu/Stone/Getty Images; pp. 7, 11, 24 (top left) © www.iStockphoto.com/Dmitry Deshevykh; pp. 16–17 © www.iStockphoto.com/Andrew Howe; pp. 20–21 Johnny Johnson/The Image Bank/Getty Images; p. 23 © www.iStockphoto.com/Tom Tietz; p. 24 (top right) Hemera/Thinkstock.

Library of Congress Cataloging-in-Publication Data

Sebastian, Emily.
  Foxes / by Emily Sebastian. — 1st ed.
       p. cm. — (Animals underground)
  Includes index.
  ISBN 978-1-4488-4953-6 (library binding) — ISBN 978-1-4488-5056-3 (pbk.) —
  ISBN 978-1-4488-5057-0 (6-pack)
  1. Foxes—Juvenile literature. I. Title. II. Series.
  QL737.C22S435 2012
  599.775—dc22

2010050093

Manufactured in the United States of America

CPSIA Compliance Information: Batch #WS11PK: For Further Information contact Rosen Publishing, New York, New York at 1-800-237-9932

CONTENTS

Foxes are part of the dog family.
They are smart!

There are several kinds of foxes. **Red foxes** are the most common foxes.

Swift foxes live on the Great Plains. These are grasslands in the middle of North America.

Arctic foxes have white coats in the winter. In the summer, their coats turn gray or brown.

Female foxes are called vixens. Males are known as dogs, tods, or reynards.

Foxes eat many foods. They may eat eggs, bugs, rabbits, mice, and berries.

Foxes stand very still when they see animals. Then they jump on them.

Baby red foxes have dark fur. Baby foxes are called kits or cubs.

Newborn cubs drink their mothers' milk. Later on, their parents bring the cubs food.

Cubs stay near their families' **dens**. They play with each other and with older foxes.

23

Words to Know

arctic fox

den

red fox

swift fox

Index

Web Sites

Due to the changing nature of Internet links, PowerKids Press has developed an online list of Web sites related to the subject of this book. This site is updated regularly. Please use this link to access the list:

www.powerkidslinks.com/anun/foxes/